The Best of
H.M.Bateman
The Tatler Cartoons 1922-26

Foreword by Mark Boxer

THE BODLEY HEAD
LONDON

British Library   Cataloguing in Publication Data

Bateman, H.M.
The best of H.M. Bateman: the Tatler cartoons 1922-26.
1. English wit and humour, Pictorial
I. Title
741.5'942   NC1479

ISBN 0-370-31070-5
ISBN 0-370-3187-X Pbk

Printed in Great Britain for The Bodley Head Ltd
32 Bedford Square, London WC1B 3EL
by
Wm Clowes Ltd, Beccles, Suffolk

FOREWORD

In the eighteenth century, engravings of Gillray's cartoons were so popular that they were rented out overnight like latter-day videos. Grandees would buy them in St. James's; but those lower down the social scale hired them to entertain their friends. Over a hundred years later reproductions of H M Bateman's 'The Man Who' series could be bought for 10/6 from the offices of *The Tatler* in the Strand. Bateman himself was paid the amazing sum of £200 by *The Tatler* for some of these drawings. This was the equivalent of the yearly stipend of a curate. Framed in *passé-partout* and often hung in the dens and cloakrooms of suburban England they took pride of place next to the illustration of a goose inspecting the private parts of a boy under a sun hat. They both provided what the British wanted from their artists, a minor conversational piece. But on a more flattering level the humorous drawings of Bateman were almost as important to the public in a pre-television age as the comedy of John Cleese and Eric Morecambe was fifty years later. Bateman's success was such that he was able to retire in his mid-forties and could afford to spend the rest of his life indulging his life-long ambition to be a painter.

Bateman at his best was an extremely skilled, humorous artist. But the reason for his extraordinary success was probably based on the ordinariness of his subject matter. Bateman was *par excellence* the cartoonist of suburban life. Those who have read the work of Gissing will know how the new railways in the early years of the present century combined with a burgeoning middle class to create suburbia. Bateman spent his formative years in Romford and Honour Oak. As his work developed it embraced all the impedimenta of suburban life: the golf clubs and golf courses of southern England, the *thé dansant*, musical evenings, etiquette, the minutiae of social standing, the risks of marriage for a man, the stark necessity of marriage for a woman. Then with the proliferation of the motor car and his own rising income after the First World War Bateman's horizons broadened. Grand dinners, the Season, plush hotels, furriers, even yachts crept into his drawings, though he was always an outsider in the world of Rotten Row and the Pump Room.

The series of drawings which made him famous, 'The Man Who' series, was started in a small way around 1911, but they only got into their stride in the early Twenties. Earlier Bateman had, more or less single-handed, developed the strip cartoon in this country, though the idea owed a considerable amount to the continental cartoonist Caran D'Ache whom Bateman greatly admired. Bateman's strip cartoons, sometimes several pages long, were mainly in black and white which *Punch* preferred. It was partly for this reason that the cartoons illustrated here, which were in colour, appeared on the centre pages of *The Tatler*, though a contributory factor may well have been the meanness of *Punch*.

During the Twenties and Thirties *The Tatler* was an extremely successful magazine with a considerable circulation; photographs of the smart set at parties and at race meetings seem to have had a hypnotic appeal in pre-television days. The newspapers of the day would devote pages to a 'society' wedding. Lady Diana Cooper was in some ways the Joan Collins of her day. In Cecil Beaton's eyes *The Tatler* was a more important and glamorous magazine than *Vogue* or any of the other social and dramatic magazines. *The Tatler* was a bastion of conventional values and Bateman's drawings about parvenu or naïve behaviour in society suited the magazine to a T. Unfortunately, *The Tatler* has gone through so many vicissitudes and owners since Bateman's day that no archives remain to illuminate his dealings with the magazine. The only concrete information I have been able to glean, apart from his impressive fee, was to discover that a drawing on the subject of Freemasonry was rejected, which would not happen today.

If Bateman's work for *The Tatler* marked the apogee of his career and made him a star (as well as putting the word 'Batemanesque' into the language), he nevertheless had an immediate success at the beginning of his career. His life story is easily told. At an early age he was embraced by the English Arts Club group which dominated the English art scene from the portals of the Sketch Club, the Chelsea Arts Club and the Savage. This rapport with older men probably prematurely aged him and distanced him from his contemporaries. He was a shy, introverted man and in some ways was a rather tragic one. Like many outstanding cartoonists (Dyson, Low) his early life was spent in Australia. His domineering mother insisted they return to England and encouraged her son to go to Art School after eliciting the support of Phil May. Bateman's decision to become a humorous artist rather than a 'serious' one caused him some distress and probably was the reason for his nervous breakdown at the age of twenty-one. The First World War revealed him to be, in his own phrase, 'a hopeless dud' as a soldier and he spent most of the War as a civilian and semi-invalid. For a conventional man this was clearly the stuff of serious trauma. Bateman thereafter led a rather isolated life. In true suburban fashion he kept himself to himself. He married late and the marriage didn't last. His wife was clearly convivial as well as a cut above him socially. He retreated further and further away from 'civilization', ending his days alone on the island of Gozo. Many of his later years were spent carrying on a ridiculous and sad battle with the Inland Revenue.

There are several ways of categorizing cartoonists; but the main division seems to me to be between those who draw with deadly accuracy people and their habitat and those who invent a world of their own. In the former category I put Giles, Osbert Lancaster, Belcher, Pont, Anton, Peter Arno and Saxon, to name but a few. In the second category you enter a looking-glass world where life is recognizable but has been brilliantly distorted. At the peak of this group stand such figures as Saul Steinberg, Charles Addams, Heath Robinson and Bateman. After

The Man Who Watches The Speedometer

seeing old American houses through the eyes of Charles Addams for example, clapboard never seems quite so innocent ever again. On a lower echelon, where whimsy has taken over from true fantasy, there are such popular cartoonists as Roland Emett and Peynet. Bateman's originality is generally agreed to be based on the way he drew people not as they *looked* but as they *felt*. If we are embarrassed we say we feel very small. Bateman took such a phrase literally and drew a lieutenant who, on eating the colonel's savoury, shrinks to the size of a canapé. On one level Bateman's cartoons have a crudeness and vulgarity which echoes the work of Donald McGill, the perpetrator of the seaside postcard. But on another level he invests a conventional scene with a vein of surrealism and a use of the grotesque which makes his work unique.

Apart from his development of the strip cartoon (which later was to be driven into the ground by the relentless pen of Fougasse) he was also responsible for another remarkable innovation. This was his use of a frieze at the bottom of some of his drawings where the central figures in the main cartoon are brilliantly elaborated (see fig 1). He also employed a device I have not seen used earlier: an infuriated colonel on a putting green issues from his mouth an oath of tangible and monstrous proportions which is beyond words (see fig 2). This pre-dates Saul Steinberg's elaborate and elegant use of the same idea by three decades.

Like many outstanding cartoonists, Bateman created his own cast of characters. He is probably responsible for the national stereotype of the apoplectic colonel whose lineage leads to Low's Colonel Blimp. Bateman also had an acute eye in his early career for both amateur and professional musicians who must have been both the bane and solace of Edwardian life. He also had a good line in overfed suburban

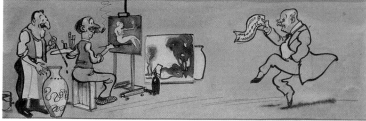

matrons. But above all he had a genius for drawing the appalling red-faced businessmen of his period. With their terrible moustaches and shiny black hair matching their patent leather shoes they were the epitome of The Man Who Had Done Well Out Of The War.

Apart from their standing as classics of humorous art the cartoons in this collection will also be appreciated now for their description of the decor and architecture of suburban England. Bateman's ability as a 'straight' artist, which sadly resulted in rather mundane water colours and oils, served him in good stead here. Bateman's most fruitful period covered the rise of the motor car, the cloche and the charabanc, the emergence of Woolworths and the last days of the Spa. His 'sets' make an accurate background for the scenes played before them, whether it is Lloyds, or a suburban kitchen, or the ballroom in which the Etonian refuses to play nuts and may.

Most cartoons have an element of the theatrical. The very shape of the traditional cartoon echoes the proscenium arch. The characters in cartoons have to project themselves; many situations and gag lines could just as well be used in a theatrical revue or on the music hall stage. Bateman's cartoons in particular have a theatrical dimension. Like many other cartoonists, in drawing an exaggerated stance or contorted face he would act it out himself at the drawing board. Surprisingly for a shy man, Bateman in his youth thought of going on the stage; and later on he did a stint as a theatrical caricaturist for *The Bystander* and *The Sketch*. But with 'The Man Who' series Bateman entered the traditions of pure farce. Indeed in many cases his characters are

fig 1 (left), Genuine Antiques
fig 2 (right), The New Word in Golf

beyond speech. The comparable skill in the theatre is that of mime.

Many of Bateman's drawings seem to be inspired by an anger of centrifugal proportions. But surprisingly it appears as if his own sympathy in 'The Man Who' series often lay with the figure who has made the gaffe. His real scorn seems to be aimed at the appalled onlookers. In the excellent biography of Bateman by Anthony Anderson (to whom I am much indebted for many of the facts in this essay) there is a revealing description of Bateman walking out of a grand city dinner in the middle of a speech by Lord Astor, no less. Bateman was clearly capable of his own form of bravery and unconventionality. The crux to Bateman's cartoons here is that psychologically he was an outsider. He drew insiders, but he was not one of them. By this time in his life Bateman didn't like people very much. This was probably the source of his inspiration; but exploring such a vein in his own psyche was at a considerable cost to the man himself.

Like most great or seminal cartoonists whose work transcends their own period, Bateman's cartoons rely primarily on the humour of the drawings rather than on the caption. When Bateman first started out as a cartoonist the typical *Punch* cartoon of the day carried considerable excess baggage. Each piece of dialogue was usually accompanied by a bracketed description of the participants' feelings or attitudes which should have been indicated by the drawing. (I often suspect they were written in by prosy sub-editors trying to get in on the act.) The drawings, weighed down with heavy cross-hatching, leaned heavily on illustration techniques. The drawings themselves were seldom funny. In contrast, for their time Bateman's drawings were marvellously economical. There was nothing in the drawing that didn't need to be there. Although he didn't go as far as Pont and Fougasse were able to go later in leaving things out, nevertheless he pointed the way for several latter-day cartoonists who are greatly indebted to him. He produced works of humorous art where the classic *Punch* cartoon was no more than an illustrated anecdote. But perhaps most important of all he developed a brilliant way of drawing people which wonderfully parodied their body language and encapsulated their feelings in a highly dramatic manner. In many instances Bateman's drawings should be seen as the pen and ink equivalent of the routines of Chaplin and Jacques Tati.

Mark Boxer
January 1987

THE COMMANDER-IN-CHIEF'S TRUMPETER SOUNDS THE "DISMISS" IN ERROR

THE CROUPIERS WHO SHOWED SIGNS OF EMOTION

THE UMPIRE WHO CONFESSED HE WASN'T LOOKING!

THE DÉBUTANTE

DISCOVERY OF A DANDELION ON THE CENTRE COURT AT WIMBLEDON

A COWES NIGHTMARE — THE UNWELCOME GUEST

THE MAN WHO THREW A SNOWBALL AT ST. MORITZ

THE MAN WHO STOLE THE PRIZE MARROW

THE DIRT-TRACK RIDER WHO APPEARED IN ROTTEN ROW

THE HORSE THAT TOOK THE WRONG TURNING – AT EPSOM

THE FAVOURITE WINS

THE MAN WHO CREPT INTO THE ROYAL ENCLOSURE IN A BOWLER

THE MAN WHO BID HALF-A-GUINEA AT TATTERSALL'S

THE HUNTSMAN WHO TANGLED HIS CROP

CRUEL TO BE KIND

BEAGLING!

"THE GAME THAT WOULDN'T PLAY THE GAME."

VERY WELL MEANT

THE LIFEGUARDSMAN WHO DROPPED IT

BEHIND THE SCENES AT WELLINGTON BARRACKS

"STAND EASY."

THE GUARDS BATHE

THE MAN WHO BATHED FROM THE STEPS OF THE ROYAL YACHT SQUADRON

THE SECOND-LIEUTENANT WHO JOINED HIS REGIMENT COMPLETE WITH WIFE

THE SECOND LIEUTENANT WHO TOOK THE C.O.'S SAVOURY

"AND NOW, DEAR ADMIRAL, TELL US ABOUT THE BATTLE OF JUTLAND."

THE CURATE WHO SAW RED

THE MAN WHO ASKED FOR A DOUBLE SCOTCH IN THE GRAND PUMP-ROOM AT BATH

THE GIRL WHO ORDERED A GLASS OF MILK AT THE CAFÉ ROYAL

THE MAN WHO ASKED FOR A SECOND HELPING AT A CITY COMPANY DINNER

THE MAN WHO LIT HIS CIGAR BEFORE THE ROYAL TOAST

THE SHAREHOLDER WHO DARED TO CRITICIZE THE CHAIRMAN'S REPORT

INDUCING THE CHAIRMAN TO FACE THE SHAREHOLDERS

THE UNDERWRITER WHO MISSED THE TOTAL LOSS

A VENTRILOQUIST AT CHRISTIE'S

THE ETONIAN WHO WAS ASKED TO PLAY "NUTS AND MAY"

THE PARENTS WHO CAME BY CHARABANC

THE WOMAN WHO SPENT £10 IN A WOOLWORTH STORE

THE SHOP ASSISTANT WHO LOST HIS TEMPER

THE LADY WHO ASKED FOR "RABBIT"

HE HAD INSURED AGAINST TWINS

COOK DOESN'T FEEL LIKE IT

THE MAN WHO GAVE COOK NOTICE

THE THIRD ENCORE

THE VOICE THAT FILLED THE ALBERT HALL

A SLIGHT MISUNDERSTANDING WITH THE TILL

THE CAR THAT TOUCHED A POLICEMAN

THE ADMISSION

A LITTLE DISINFECTANT

THE CAD WHO WAS IMPROPERLY DRESSED ON THE LIDO

THE LAST TROUT

THE MEMBER OF THE BEAUTY CHORUS WHO GOT OUT OF STEP

The Publishers wish to thank Mr Richard Webb for his gracious permission to reproduce 'The New Word in Golf'.